EMERGENCY PLANNING FOR

YOUR ORGANISATION

BY

ANDRÉ NEL

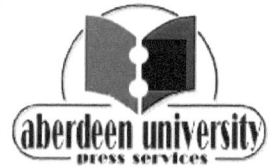

Published by Aberdeen University Press Services.

Printed in the United States of America
ISBN: 978-0-6152-1219-7

This book is printed on 6" x 9", perfect binding, 60# cream interior paper, black and white interior ink, 100# white exterior paper, full-color exterior ink. Prices are subject to change.

Cover Title Designed by Aberdeen University Press Services.

EMERGENCY PLANNING FOR YOUR ORGANISATION

First Edition
André Nel

*"My thoughts are always with the fire fighters
that gave their lives in the World Trade Center (WTC)
event that changed the way we think about
emergency planning".*
*"They were at the scene because they were
doing their job, as well trained professionals".*

- André Nel

TABLE OF CONTENTS

INTRODUCTION

1. Introduction

    a.   What has occurred?

    b.   What degree do these occurrences occur?

    c.   What is an emergency?

    d.   Factual evidence

a. What has occurred?

Through the ages we have seen and certainly witnessed many catastrophes as well as events that have changed lives forever as well as, in some cases time.

***Just a few to mention*:-**

In the Ancient times there were many villages destroyed by Fire.

London's great fire of 1666

The USA earthquakes in San Francisco

First and Second World War

Then, in our resent life time:-

The Tsunami's

World Trade Centre

Chernobyl Nuclear disaster

Ferry disasters

Australian Wild bush fires

Lockerby Airline bombing

These are just a few to mention, there have been many more, and the sad thing is there are still more that will occur maybe in our lifetime or indeed our children's life time.

b. What degree do these occurrences occur?

Through many evident findings and the actual events that have lead up to disasters or emergencies, we find that there have been many degrees at which the loss of some form has taken place.

The below facts are:-

i. *A single Gail force wind may costs Millions of Revenue in the short term as well as in the long term.*

ii. *A shoot out at a school may leave many families and people with Psychological problems, which will cost time, money and repairing as well as future costly elements.*

iii. *A plane crash whether at an Airport or in the country, seems to escalate into billions of revenue, as we see the legal cases against certain liable parties concerned, the environment may suffer and the rehabilitation will cost much more that the actual event.*

iv. *A flood may also cause severe damage even after the event has taken place.*

I will discuss the planning strategies later in the book.

c. What is an emergency?

A very debatable subject, I have had many definitions and some are found all over the world, I would like to express my views and what the others Professionals say.

"Crisis, urgent situation, disaster or tragedy" Thesaurus

My definition of an emergency is:-

"Any situation or event that may lead to a change or alter the way your organisation normally operates and needs immediate action, whether positive or negative, may be called an emergency".

André Nel 2006 (My own opinion)

Indeed there are many definitions which are correct and to the point, after all it is expressed as an event of string of events that led to the actual disaster.

I just think that in order to plan for an event, one must simply know how an emergency may affect your Organisation or Company, whether Municipal or Private, as we know an emergency may be an integrated part of events that will affect us all.

d. Factual evidence

It is very evident that after each emergency, however small or large, factual evidence always surfaces, which should make your emergency contingency plan work better. This may not always be the case, as many other aspects are not taken into account, especially when an emergency is on a large scale.

For example "How can we cover every aspect, if all the facts are not known or have been carefully covered?" If you look at the iceberg you may see only the tip and not the bigger picture?

Once you have gathered all the factual evidence, you may have to reanalyse your findings, to look outside the box, or step out of the circle and look inside "reality check".

The old *cliché* may also surface **"Don't assume/learn from your past mistakes".**

EVENTS AND INCIDENTS

2. <u>Types of incidents</u>

a. <u>Attacks</u>

I think in this day and age we simply cannot rule out attacks, as we have seen, attacks may be Biological, Physical, or Military. Each of these events may have a certain amount of long term cause for these events to take place. Nobody or Entity just wakes up one day and say" I think I will attack this target today" it just doesn't happen.

We must always look at the events that took place before an attack to actually plan against it. This may be easier said than done, I do realise it but there are elements that are seeing this attack as a prize and if it means taking out the surrounding elements, well that's ok (Collateral damage). Remember an attack is what is says "it's an attack on you, your asset or people, which in any event may be devastating to the future of your existence.

b. <u>Common acts</u>

A common act may include an individual or events that led to the emergency in the first place. You must understand that a <u>common act</u> may occur anytime.

The famous story of the "Boy in Holland, who placed his finger in the dyke to prevent the whole dam wall from giving way". It reiterates the importance of having Hazard Identification Risk Assessments (HIRA'S)as well as knowing your risk areas to prevent the event from occurring in a larger and more devastating peril, which alternately leads to losing life's.

<u>Common acts</u> will be the human interface which has some bearing towards and emergency. A small incident may lead to a large incident which in turn is called a holistic disaster. The ignorance or misinformed person may be the reason for event occurring.

Andrè Nel © 2008

c. Miscellaneous

There are many miscellaneous incidents that we see especially today, they are:-

Revenue restraints

Old technology

Human factors

Accidents

Process mishaps

Legal compliance not being met

Criminal activities

3. Emergency AIDS

a. People

b. Resources

c. Assistance

d. Communications

a. People

I think that people are one of your greatest assets in any business today, as a computer will simplify your operation but will have no emotional or intelligence linked towards the human "x"- factor. In many Organizations you will see that the Human resources component will always be the force that drives other components and elements to reach your objectives.

The people in your emergency plan have to be one of your top priorities for your emergency plan to be carried out successfully. The people you have onboard have to be trained and well informed especially in the emergency evacuation and survival arena. Without your people's reactions you would simply have an normal emergency and would as we say in the fire fraternity " leave the building to burn" which makes sense if you have all the souls safe and you have done what you could, you have minimised the loss of life.

b. Resources

This is an important piece of the puzzle as you would need many types of resources to achieve at least half of your goal and that is to get people alive safely. Resources may have influences in the type of operation and core business of your Organisation. The resources that I have found very important in planning against any disasters are:-

People

Vehicles (trucks, transport, air support)

Mechanical machinery

Power back up support systems

Food resources for your workers at the scene

Heavy hydraulic equipment

Emergency Funds

Rescue equipment (Power tools, cranes bull dozers and lifting gear

Medical resources

Town/municipality/county resource back up

Geological resources

Global resources (Other assistance from other countries as well as technology)

Police resources

Medical standby resources

Command and control

Military or defence Departments

Your own resources for your Organisation

c. <u>Assistance</u>

This topic is very wide and may include your department to make certain decisions with regard to including all the customers, role players, clients as well as neighbouring agencies to buy into the emergency planning culture, as yes will affect all in the area and beyond.

The assistance may come in different forms such as:-

Military assistance

Police assistance

Medical assistance

Local and international first aid organisations

Companies

Government

Hospitals

Schools

Churches

These are just a few; there are many other ones you could use. One has to simply benchmark and take notice of what other Organisations are doing to plan for emergencies?

d. **Communications**

The communications is one of the most important issues that form part of an emergency plan. The fact is without communications you may find yourself in a bit of a pickle.

Communications may include:-

Satellite platforms

Hand held phones/two way radios

Deck phone systems

Landline systems

Cellular networks

Certain emergency frequencies (Ultra High/low)

Aviation communication systems

Integrated Communications Systems

The communication systems you choose is entirely up to the user, although a word of caution, a communication system must be able to:-

Be used for the full duration of the emergency expected.

Have back-up power and utilities

May be integrated for all users

Be communicated to all the role players concerned and must involve training with these communication systems

Your network users must be competent in the use of these systems.

Also remember to consult the Military/Aviation Authorities in your area to liaison any illegal frequencies that may be used   by   Organisations

EQUIPMENT

4. **Equipment**

   a. **First aid**

   First aid equipment is a vital part of one's emergency planning as this equipment may be used at the scene as well as serve as the first line of defence to assist those who are injured and may need the help. It <u>must also</u> be mentioned that although the emergency first aid equipment such as first aid kits, medical and supporting equipment may not help when there is a large fire or sudden explosion causing harm to all in the inner circle, it is important to have this equipment in the vicinity, as this will be of assistance to all the patients that need primary or secondary medical treatment.

   After all, in an emergency you may be in a situation where you are trapped and may only be rescued days later, this is first aid equipment may be helpful. There are certain causes of death in the first hours of an emergency that may be a vital statistic to saving lives. As we see that death may be caused by:-

   Trauma/which leads to shock

   Bleeding

   Internal bleeding

   Crushing injuries

   Head injuries

   Chest injuries

   And other

   Remember to have the first aid equipment in place is well, but are the persons trained to use this equipment? Is the question?

   b. **Fire Equipment**

   Fire equipment is only used as a first aid fire fighting tool and must not be seen as the ultimate safety devise in emergency situations, as the fire equipment is dead unless used correctly and positively. I am not speaking about the fire suppression systems that are required to be installed in a building to be compliant. I am merely saying that Portable fire fighting equipment should be installed in each place of trade/marketing/services/warehouses etc. The fact that it is in place, is good but however will not be effective if the user is not trained and found competent to use it effectively.

Fire equipment is listed as the following:-

Portable fire extinguishers (all types)

Fire blankets

Fire fighting hose reels

Fire Hoses

Fire hydrants

Fire alarm systems

FIRE SUPPRESSION SYSTEMS ARE:-

(Normally 24 hours fire protection surveillance systems)

Water Sprinkler systems

Foam systems

Deluge systems (Flooding)

Water jet protection systems

Secondary back-up systems

(These systems serve as fire protection guards)

Fire Dampers

Ventilation systems

Emergency automatic Fire shutter doors

Emergency stairs

Emergency escape routes and exits

Emergency steel escapes

c. Emergency equipment

This equipment is normally your:-

Emergency backup lighting/Generators

Power supplies

Automatic alarms

Self contained breathing apparatus (SCUBA)

Rescue lines

Communication systems

Personal protective equipment, such as:-

Helmets

Gloves

Face masks

Shields

Aprons

Reflective jackets

Safety harnesses

Glow cones/safety cones

Danger/barrier tape

Ear muffs/protectors

Safety boots

Fire fighting safety gear

There are many more that are in practice today. these are just the essentials

Remember to do the job effectively you need the right tools the first time.

TRAINING ANDAWARENEWSS

5.   **Training and Awareness**

a. **People assets**

Without recognising the importance of your people you will certainly loss the fight.   The proven fact is Training and awareness for all employees, customers, clients and related parties with regards to emergency preparedness will yield good results before, during and after an emergency.

Note: To have a safety emergency contingency awareness training in place is all well, but if you do not have this as your living workable document, you are lost.

b. **Knowledge**

The great saying "Knowledge is Power" is very true, as your work force needs to have the tools to maintain and provide a service when it counts.

The emergency planning tool is empowerment to ensure you may reach your emergency planning goal. And that is to have a plan that works through-out the systems. One has to also benchmark to ensure that you stay current and active as the race towards a almost faultless emergency plan (Which I think, is quite unattainable at this stage as there are always new ideas and methodologies on the horizon.) It does not help to have all the management tools and [people skills if the knowledge levels are not present.

c.   **Programs**

"A good program has got to be challenged to keep it good".
By André Nel 2007

A program with all the "*bells and whistles*" may look impressive, but may not even reach 20% of its objectives in an emergency, be careful for these traps?

An emergency program has to be adaptable, be able to have room for improvement and also accommodate new updates. Programs do work and must be in line to be audited. They may also have to be generic to accommodate all the role players' needs.

d. Valid updated programs

This may be the factor that may have to be watched closely to ensure that your emergency contingency planning does not become outdated, which has occurred in many Countries in the World. The common practice is to have these plans reviewed as often as twice a year depending on the type of exposures and risks one has to deal with.

MUTUAL AID

6. Mutual Aid

Mutual aid should be a basic need for every Organisations fundamental as History has taught us in the past. The reason to have mutual aid is to:-

Build a relationship before the incident

Encourage new ideas

Integration between parties

Share all interests and assets

To make a mark in your community/social responsibility

Environmental responsibility

Ensuring growth and stability for the future

Making a difference

a. Integrated Systems

A Mutual aid system should be an integrated system at all costs, as you will find that when an incident occurs? Many organisations will work on their own and NOT as a Team, this may cause major problems. The main break down is when it comes to the communication systems and the "who *is responsible for what, scenario*?"

b. Financial planning

This is the most important aspect of the emergency contingency planning, as if your management does not buy into your concept, you may as well close shop. The prove has been to many times there is a financial issue when the time comes to the planning, as Organisation will argue the fact that they have put enough funds into the emergency fund to sustain whatever emergency is anticipated. This is a wrong concept as we know all thing increase as time goes by. We need to Plan financially to back-up our Goals and actions especially at the time if the emergency. Financial planners must also be involved in the planning stages to ensure they are on the same page as the executers of the operations. All the agreements and service level agreements must be in place before the disaster occurs, as we know

"*if it was not documented, it did not happen*".

A good financial plan will spell out the benefits as well as the entire positive returns one will have, especially knowing you can sleep well at night, knowing that you have taken all the financial steps to prevent a less effective arena.

BUILDING YOUR EMERGENCY CONTINGENCY PLAN

7. Building your emergency contingency plan

The most important thing to remember is that your plan may not necessary suite the next Organisation, and that the uniqueness may still be evident. To establish your emergency plan the following ideas have been formulated to give you a better idea:-

a. Stake holders

You must involve all the stakeholders, whether large or small. Often these stakeholders will bring good ideas to the table, which will also have an impact of your plan.

b. Effects (worst case scenario)

The normal planning will focus on the worst case scenario that may influence your organisation. But what is the worst case scenario? Maybe a storm, attack, fire, water etc. You must use the total scope of your scenarios to cover most of the areas concerned.

c. A live working document

This is very important, because if you have a well presented document and it does not work in reality, you have lost the plot and the game. To ensure your plan is a live working document you need to do the following:-

Test

Have practical drills

Involve everyone on the plan (Role players)

Be evaluated by a third party

Be measured against another plan

Have post mortems to discuss alternatives, especially if there were problem areas.

d. Legislation

In most cases before you plan for an emergency you must look at:-

Current Legislation (In your Country)

Make sure you are in within your boundaries

Consult Environmental issues

Look at World leads hip programs that may be instituted in your area

Be compliant in your documentation and systems

Look at your policies and procedures within the scope of practice, especially when dealing with other parties

e.   Management systems

The management systems you may use may vary from place to place.   There are very similarities with many of them. You have to ensure the Management systems work for you and if it works, keep using it?   By managing people you are providing them with tools and power to work for your plan.

f.   Bench marks

The benchmarks have worked for several Organisations.   It is a good practice to benchmark but remember to use the correct benchmark that may have a similar core business and not something way out of scope.

g. Testing system

As mentioned before, there are many ways to test your systems to see if you are really reaching your objectives.

h.   Review

The review is important to ensure that you have covered all or most of the grey area in your emergency planning.   It is good practice to review your plans, to ensure *compliance, relevance, new technology*, updates and many more areas are checked and maintained.

FUTURE 21st CENTURY BUILDINGS

8. Future 21st Century buildings

a. The new generation buildings

b. Making way for the thinking philosophy

c. The way forward

a. The new generation buildings

During the past decade, there have been many new buildings that have been build through-out the world; we see these buildings emerging in modern cities as well as all the stadia and world sports events. These buildings have intelligent systems installed (*by man, I may add*) to manage and cover all aspects of safety/fire suppression systems/security and maintenance systems. We see for an example:-

There are buildings that will react to certain climate change (temperature/ pressures/ weather). They simply will close off windows, take the glare out of windows, when the sun is too hot or when the rain starts to pour down. In the fire suppression systems we see that the computer will be backed up by power systems or simply UPS (Uninterrupted Power Supply) that will react in a fire situation or create a system to react if the area is affected by change.

b. Making way for thinking Philosophy

The building we are talking about should not be farfetched or unrealistic, we should embrace the idea that in the near future we will indeed have buildings that will think for us and make decisions, especially in the emergency evacuation field of study. And why not as we reach the age of beyond we see that motor vehicle and houses have the ability to tell you when to drive, park, close the doors and of course the best of all, just tune in and you can start your bath water and lights on before you even get home, now this is the thinking technology we are talking and should be looking beyond.

c. The way forward

We can believe in the new age, but the truth still remains we have to accept the fact that each time there is new technology a new technique will follow. The facts are we are still humans and humans are always finding new ways to make things easier and less complex, this is our Universe and we should embrace new safer methods that will give us the edge it only takes time.

STUDY RESULTS AND FINDINGS

9. **Study Results and Findings**

**EMERGENCY EVACUATION
QUESTIONNAIRE**

**Please answer these short questions as honest as possible,
just a mark for a <u>YES</u> or a <u>NO</u> answer.**

		YES/NO	
1.	Do you know what to do in an emergency?		
2.	Do you know where your assembly point/area is?		
3.	Have you received any formal training in emergency evacuating?		
4.	Have you heard the emergency alarm in your area?		
5.	Do you know where to find the emergency telephone numbers?		
6.	Have you been involved in an evacuation?		
7.	Are you confident to evacuate now?		
8.	Do you know who your evacuation or health & safety marshal is?		

Thank you for participating

Questionnaire Results

Overall Statistics for Answers

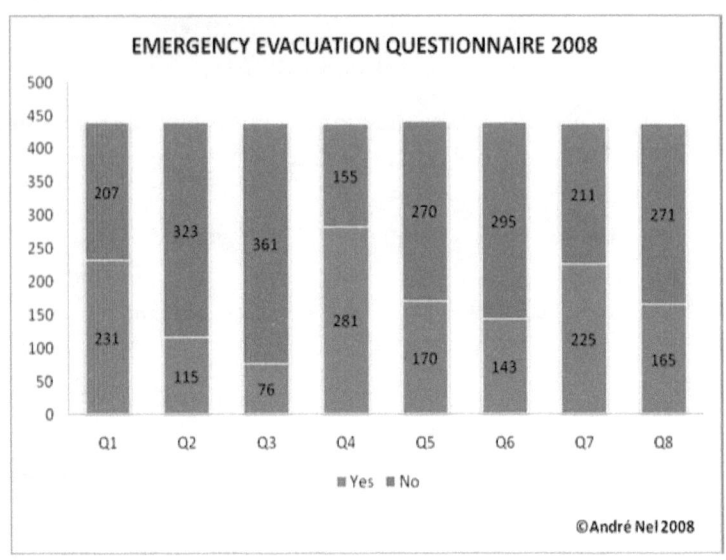

Graph depicting Yes answers

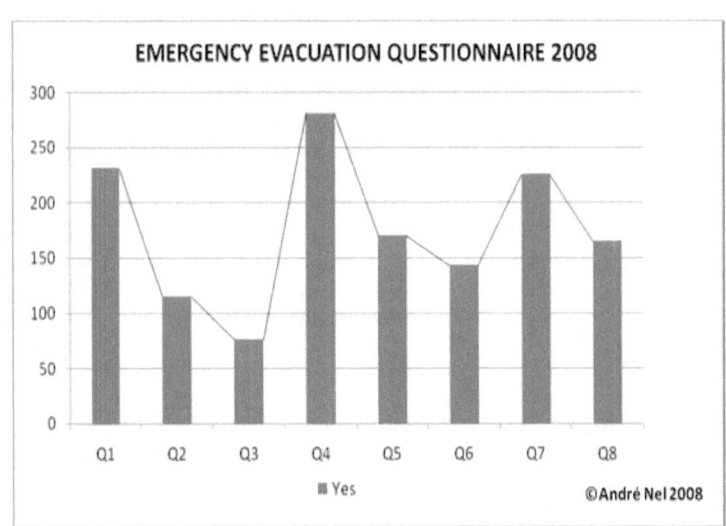

Graph Depicting No Answers

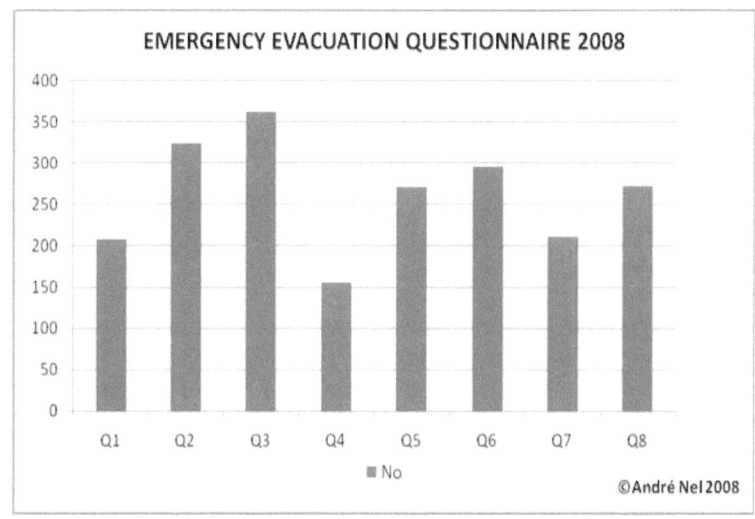

EMERGENCY EVACUATION QUESTIONNAIRE 2008

© André Nel 2008

The following percentages were worked out according to the results gathered and processed

In Question one (1) the following Question was asked:
"**Do you know what to do in an emergency**"?
It was found that 47,58% answered no they did not know what to do in an emergency, And 53.10% answered Yes they did know what to do?

In Question two (2) the following Question was asked:
"**Do you know where your assembly point/area is** "?
It was found that 74.25% answered No they did not know where the assembly point was, And 26.43% answered Yes they did know where the assembly points are?

In Question three (3) the following Question was asked:
"**Have you received any formal training in emergency evacuating**"?
It was found that 82.96% answered No they did not receive any sort of training or awareness, And 17.47% answered Yes they did have some sort of training?

In Question four (4) the following Question was asked:

"Have you heard the emergency alarm in your area"?

It was found that 35.63% answered No they did not hear the emergency alarm before, And 64.59% answered Yes they did indeed hear the emergency alarm?

In Question five (5) the following Question was asked:
"Do you know where to find the emergency telephone numbers"?
It was found that 62.06% answered No they did not know where to find the emergency telephone numbers, And 39.08% answered Yes they did know where to find them?

In Question six (6) the following Question was asked:
"Have you been involved in an evacuation"?
It was found that 67.81% answered No they were never involved in an emergency evacuation, And 32.87% answered Yes they did know what to do?

In Question seven (7) the following Question was asked:
"Are you confident to evacuate now"?
It was found that 48.50% answered No they were not confident to evacuate, And 51.72% answered Yes they were confident to evacuate?

In Question eight (8) the following Question was asked:
"Do you know who your evacuation or health & safety marshal is"?
It was found that 62.29% answered No they did not know who their evacuation or health and safety marshal was?, And 37.93% answered Yes they did know?

Final notes of findings

It is quite evident that people do not know where to assemble in times of emergency evacuation; this is a very serious observation as this may lead to confusion and even loss of lives Emergency evacuation training is also lacking especially in the corporate world due to time restrains and lack of information. People have also had little to do with evacuations, this is evident. *(Question 2/3)* There are many borderline answers, but the worrying part is that the No answers are very high compared to the no answers.

Possible solutions and recommendations

Emergency evacuation and planning should be communicated by all Management levels as well as up vertical and horizontal communications. Emergency awareness training and programs should be maintained at all cost. The emergency evacuation drills should be practised at least twice a year and also communicated to the new employees. Any Organisation should buy into this safety culture to be prepared at all times, especially in times of emergencies for this plan to be successful you have to keep it updated and make sure all your staff are trained, especially the people with disabilities.

MAKE SURE YOU ARE NOT LEFT BEHIND

<u>Emergency Evacuation model</u>

This emergency evacuation model is a working tool that may provide direction and insight to end-users

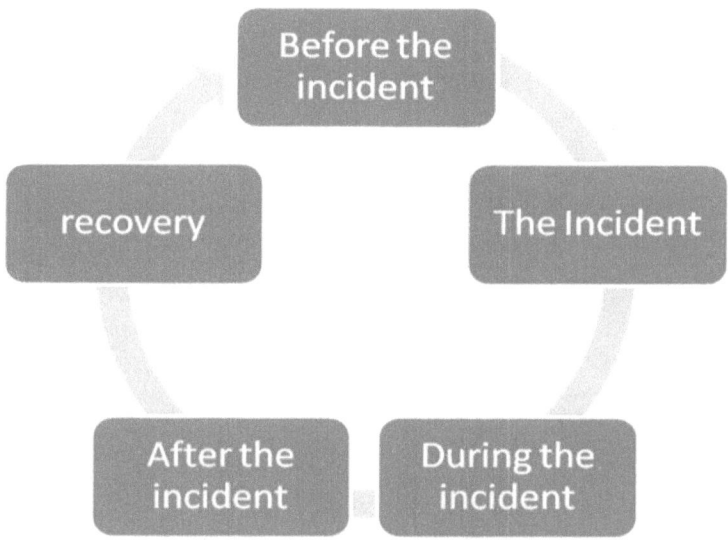

Preparing for an Emergency Evacuation

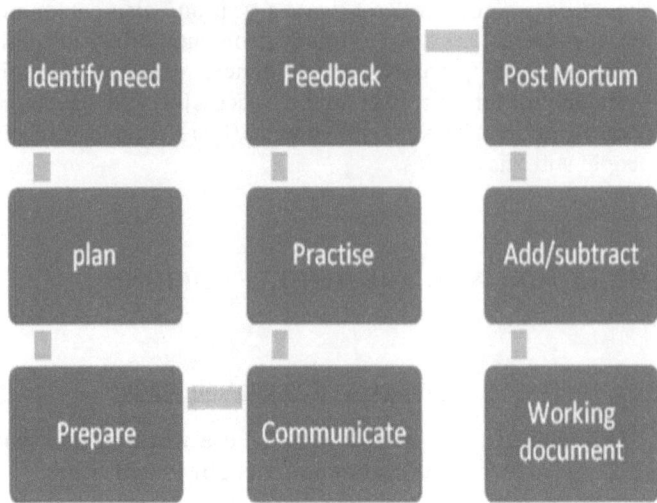

APPENDIX – I

References & Bibliography

References

The mass Psychology of disasters and Mass evacuations a research report and implications for practice by Dr's John Drury and Chris Cocking Department of Psychology University of Sussex (UK)

Guideline for Emergency Evacuations

Johannesburg Metro Fire Safety Department

The Occupational Health and Safety Act 85 of 1993 (South Africa)

The South African National Building regulations SANS Code 10400

Other relevant Emergency Preparedness Policies

Internet bibliography

Emergency Planning "Google Search"

Emergencies & Workplace Safety "Yahoo Search"

Magazine Bibliography

American Fire Journals

Glossary

"Emergency" *Any situation or event that may lead to an immediate action, whether positive or negative, may be called an emergency*

"Emergency plans" *Any plans drawn up in a document form that may serve an Organisation for emergency plan.*

"HIRA" *A Hazard Identification Risk Assessments.*

"Helmets" *Any form of protection for the head.*

"Gloves" *Any form of protection for the hand, either leather or other material designed to protect the hands.*

"Face masks" *A protection cover (mask) for the nose and mouth, to prevent any hazardous or dangerous substance, dust, fumes or harmful bacteria from entering the mouth or nasal passages.*

"Shields" *A form of cover that will shield a human against any harmful substance.*

"Aprons" *A form of protection that covers the front of the body.*

"Reflective jackets" *A jacket that is visible and may be seen at night and is reflective to any form of light.*

"Safety harnesses" *A body harness that serves the purpose of preventing a person from falling from a height.*

"Glow cones/safety cones" *A plastic conical device used to warn people of an unsafe area or condition, normally used to warn vehicle traffic or corded off an accident scene. Usually these cones are reflective or glow in the dark concept.*

"Danger/barrier tape" *Any tape that is used to corded off an area of concern and to warn of the danger in that particular area, this tape is used at police, Fire and ambulance departments to ensure no-body tampers with the evidence or scene.*

"Ear muffs/protectors" *A device that is approved by an Authority to protect the ears against noise usually against high decibels.*

"Safety boots" *Foot wear that has a protection steel toe cap or leather or synthetic material that will protect the feet against an object that might otherwise injure the foot.*

"Fire fighting safety gear" *Any fire retardant fire gear which is tested to with stand an amount of heat, this fire gear may be bunker trousers, jacket, gloves, flash hood or other special fire gear.*

Index

About Author

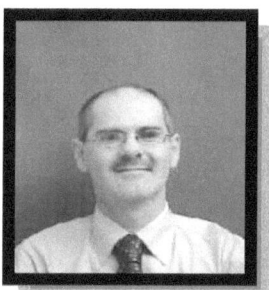

Andre was born in East London in South Africa in 1963; Andre started his emergency fire fighting career at the East London Airport Fire and Rescue services in 1982. After 7 years Andre Joined a Petrochemical Company as a Senior Fire Fighter. Andre was involved in Fire/Safety Training for Fire Fighters as well as clients. He then took up a post of Chief Fire Officer at Virginia Airport (Natal coast South Africa) where he managed the Airport Fire and Rescue Services.

Andre then took up a post in the South African Air Force as a Fire Instructor, he spend five (5) years in the Fire Instruction role, where he was involved in developing learning material and Fire Fighters careers. He then became a specialist in Aviation Fire and Rescue techniques, especially in the Sub African Climate; he also was involved in the Hazardous Material incident Management systems. In Andre's fifteen (15) years service in the South African Air Force he obtained the rank of Warrant Officer and had the privilege in training the South African President's Flight attendants and crew in Emergency and evacuation procedures involving the Boeing Business Jet (BBJ 737-800), which is now in operation. Andre has also visited other Countries in Africa.

Andre has been an EMT and has been involved in many emergency planning projects, which has come quite useful in his endeavours and expanding his knowledge in the emergency arena. Andre has been involved in International safety Conferences as a guest speaker with regards to safety/fire/aircraft safety procedures.

Andre is now also a qualified Occupational Health and Safety Practitioner and works for a Corporate Company in Johannesburg South Africa.

Andre is married to his wife Donita and has two children Tarryn and Jean-Pierre.

Andre enjoys reading listening to music and loves watching movies. Andre loves aviation and aircraft. Andre is also in the process of writing a book about his life experiences.

NOTES